Something To Think About

Inspirational Poems

By Selena Millman

First Edition

Biographical Publishing Company
Prospect, Connecticut

Something To Think About
Inspirational Poems
First Edition

Published by:
Biographical Publishing Company
35 Clark Hill Road
Prospect, CT 06712-1011
Phone: 203-758-3661   Fax: 603-853-5420   e-mail: biopub@aol.com

All rights reserved. No part of this book may be reproduced or transmitted in any form or by any means, electronic or mechanical, including photocopying, recording, or by any information storage or retrieval system without the written permission of the author, except for the inclusion of brief quotations in a review.

Copyright © 2000 by Selena Millman
First Printing 2000

PRINTED IN THE UNITED STATES OF AMERICA

Library of Congress Cataloging-in-Publication Data
Millman, Selena, 1973-
  Something to think about : inspirational poems / by Selena Millman.--
1st ed.
     p. cm.
  ISBN 1-929882-00-9 (alk. paper)
  1. Jackson, Michael, 1958---Poetry. I. Title.
  PS3563.I42285 S66 2000
  811'.6--dc21
                                                    00-008292

Table of Contents

Chapter 1
    Make A Difference Poems 4

Chapter 2
    My Feelings' Poems 19

Chapter 3
    Poems About People I Know 26

Chapter 4
    Michael Jackson Poems 36

Chapter 5
    Dreams and Other Poems 46

Chapter 6
    Character Poems 52

Chapter 7
    About The Author 74

Chapter One

Make A Difference Poems

We all can make a difference in this world!

Something To Think About

Let me give you something
To think about

Differences are superficial
What's inside is important

Why do people hurt each other
Please think hard about this

Let's help each other
We need to honestly care

Don't assume things
Take time to understand

We all can make a difference
All people can help others

Use your heart to care
Do whatever you can
Every little bit helps

How can you help
Any way you want

Did you get my point
Let's work together to help each other

Think About This

What do people care about
What do you care about

There are so many people suffering
Too much pain in the world

Why do people judge each other
Are differences really important
I don't think so

Why do we waste time and energy
Hating each little difference

Give me a break
Figure out what's important
I have already figured it out

Love is truly important
Look past the differences

Friends are very important
Let us help each other
Be there for each other

Let's make a difference
All you need is to honestly care

Love And Peace

Do you know what's important
My answer is love and peace

Give others peace
Be kind and don't judge
Everyone needs peace
Peace of mind and peace of heart

It's important to feel loved
And equally important to love others

Love makes you feel good
It's an important part of life

Keep love and peace
In your heart and mind

Tolerance

Is tolerance really so hard
How can that be

Can't we be tolerant of race
Religion and disabilities
And everything else

What's the problem here
Why do we care

Differences are superficial
Can't you see that
Don't you understand that

We must learn to let people be who they are
Without judging what they are

We Need

What do we need
I'll tell you what I think

We need to help the homeless
Feed the hungry

Give the children good homes
Never hurt the children
Please stop fighting

Don't drink and drive
It can kill you or someone else

So many are sick
In pain or alone

What's going on here
Can't we do something
We all can help somehow

Some Advice

You want some advice
Well I'll give you some
I'll give you my philosophy

Be kind to others
Be open-minded
Caring and loving

Love instead of hate
Try to help
Be there for others

You may believe
You can not do much
I believe every little bit helps

Well this is my advice
Just think about it

Problems These Days

There are so many problems
In the world these days

Why do people hate and judge
Based on differences

Let's keep an open mind
And an open heart
This will make a big difference

So many are sick and hurt
Abandoned and abused

Children with no parents
Scared and feeling alone

Drinking and driving
Addicted to drugs

Self esteem problems
Eating disorders

So much violence
Where does it come from

All these people in pain
Can't we help them
What can we do

For all those out there
I want you to know

You are not alone
People do care
And help is available

Hang In There

I know life can be tough
I feel it too

Sometimes it's so hard
And you're full of pain
That you don't know what to do

You gotta be strong
And you can't give up

I know it's hard
Very hard
I know how that feels

But somehow you got to do it
You got to get the strength

People tell me I'm strong
But I don't see it
I don't know maybe they're right

But please just hang in there
Lean on me if you need to

My Advice

Keep the faith
That's what people say

But do they realize
How hard that is
It's easy to say hard to do

You know what I'd say
I know it's tough

And I may not know what to say
But please hang in there
I'm here for you

That's my advice
It works for me

Feelings Inside

Are you sad
Feeling all alone

Like no one understands
Did you tell anyone

Tell someone you trust
Reach out
I know someone cares

Many are misunderstood
Listen and don't judge

Open your heart to care
No one is completely alone
Many people honestly care

What It Takes

What does it take
To make a difference

Mostly it takes an open mind
And a loving heart
You need to care
How hard can that be!

Hating makes everyone feel bad
Loving does the opposite
It makes you feel good

Wouldn't you rather feel good
Than bad
I know I would

Every little bit helps
I honestly believe that

Let's Think

Sometimes I just wanna tell people
Think about what you say

Do you really want to hate me
Just because I'm different

Am I black or white
Does that matter
If so, why does it

Am I really that different
Why do you think that

Well I guess you're different to me
But do you know what
I don't care

The World Today

There is so much hate
In the world today

I don't understand why
Why hate and judge

Why not take the time
To understand and care

All you need to do is be open
It helps to use your heart

It really is easy to care
At least I think so

Read what I say
And please think about it

How To Help

Some people believe
There's nothing they can do
Personally I believe everyone can do something
Even if it seems little

I am able to help a few people
All I do is listen
And let them know I sincerely care
They know I'm here for them

I am open-minded
And I truly care
I believe that's all you need to help
And to make a difference

Anyone can do it
Anyone can care
All you need is an open mind
And a loving heart

Make A Difference

We should all make a difference
If everyone did a little
It would add up to a lot

Every little bit helps
That's my belief

Sometimes just listening helps
A lot of times all you got to do is care
Honestly care

If you care you can help
All you really need is an open mind
And a loving heart

If you make a difference in one person's life
That is wonderful

If we all did that
Just imagine
What we could accomplish

What Can I Do

What can I do
To make a difference
That's what I wanna know

There are a lot of things
I believe every bit helps

You can listen to a friend in need
It may seem little
But it's important
You can make a difference
By helping your friend

You can be open-minded
Be tolerant of differences
That itself can go a long way

Think of others
Be caring
If you know someone in need
Help them

Don't believe rumors
And don't start them

Instead of hating
Try loving
Don't just pretend to care

All of this may seem little
But to me it's a lot
It can make a difference
Why not try it

Against Hate

Am I black or white
What religion or nationality
Am I or are you

Why hate what you don't know
Why judge people who are different

If they are different than you
You are different to them as well

What's important about hate
How does it make you feel

Do you hate someone
Just because they are different
If you do, why?

I'll never understand
How people can hate and judge

Differences do not matter
Not at all

People are more similar
Than different
We all need love, support, and friends

Why not take time
Try to understand

Get to know people
Never assume things

You can not see what's in a heart
Just by looking at a person

Help To Heal

Everyone counts
And everyone matters
No one is unimportant

Every person has the power
To change and make a change
If each person was open-minded
And helped only one person
This world would be a better place

I have a few friends who help me
And a couple that I can help
It feels good to help
To be cared about
And loved

Everyone likes and needs that feeling
And everyone has the power to give that feeling
If you want to Heal
You need to Love
And Don't Judge
Think About It!

Chapter Two

My Feelings' Poems

These are my personal feelings.

You And Me

Who are you to tell me what to do
Why are you better than me

Sure I'm different
Aren't we all just a little

I have my own dreams
My own beliefs and goals

I'm sure you do too
Maybe even some are the same

You won't know that
Unless you have a conversation
You got to talk to me

Maybe if you actually talk to me
You have to listen too
Maybe we're not that different

You listen to me
I promise I'll listen to you

Just get to know me
Please don't judge me

I don't judge people
It's not in my heart to judge

I would rather love others
And have others love me

I don't want to hurt anyone

I want to help people

The Way I Think

I feel like I'm alone
And I don't belong

I'm different
I don't mean on the outside
I mean on the inside

I think different
Than just about anyone I met

People take care of themselves
I want to change the world

I want to help and heal
And touch lives

I know very few like me
Maybe there are more out there
I hope there are

What's In My Heart

There are some things
I just don't understand
And I think I never will

Why do people like to judge
What they do not understand
I could never do that

It's not what's in my heart

I want to love
And be loved
I'm very open-minded
I truly and sincerely care

My dream is to make a difference
To open people's eyes
And touch their hearts

I wish people would see
Differences are not so important
There is more than that

I'd rather love and help
Not hate and judge!

Can You

Can you see what's in my heart
Do you see what I feel

Can you read my eyes
Do you know what's in my head

I think and feel many things
There are many sides to me

I want to help myself
But I also want to heal the world

I want to make a difference
And to help others

Can you see me
The real me

My Feelings

At times I feel so alone
I wonder who truly cares
I feel neglected and unloved

I have many wonderful friends
And I love them all so much

But they're all too far away
No one to hug or hold me

I want to cry
But the tears won't come
I feel my heart is broken

I try to hold on and keep the faith
But it's so hard!

Keeps Me Going

What keeps me going
I ask that a lot

My friends definitely do
They support and encourage me
I love all my friends

My writing helps
I want to touch lives

I want to make a difference
To help and heal

My dreams keep me going
They give me hope
Michael Jackson helps too

Notice Me

I heard someone ask
Where I am

Well I'm wondering something too
Did they just now notice
I have not been there

I've been here all along
Has anyone noticed

Even if I'm in the room
Most people don't notice me
Very few do

I'm quiet and shy
So I guess they think I'm not there

Thoughts In My Head

I have so many thoughts in my head
They're always there
Day and night

I think about how I feel

And how my friends feel

I think about my writing
And all my ideas

I think about dreams and wishes
What I want to come true

I think about helping
I want to make a difference

These are the thoughts in my head
Wow it's a lot

Here Alone Thinking

What can I do
To get through to you
How can I make you see how I feel

I'm here alone thinking
Do you know that

Do you know how I feel
I bet you don't
If I'm wrong tell me

I feel a lot of things
More than I'll tell you

I keep my thoughts inside
Or I write them down

Chapter Three

Poems About People I Know

These are poems
about people I love!

Dear Friends

You are all special to me
You make me so happy
Happier than you could know

Jennifer I've known you for so long
You are my first true friend

Tammy Jo I feel connected to you
I love you so much big sis
I need you in my life

Susan you're so special to me
You're an awesome singer
Te Amo Hermana

Amy you're dear to me
Tamanna you are wonderful

Hege you're the best
Mari I'm so glad we met
Kelly and Sandra
You'll always be in my heart

To my other friends
I'm sorry I can't name you all
If I did this could be too long

I love you all so much
More than I can express
More than words can say

Christina & Michael

I love you 2 so much
More than words can say
You're both special to me

Chrissy you make me happy
You make me feel loved
I love when you hug me

Mikey you make me smile
You make me laugh
You're so much fun

Being your honorary auntie
Makes me feel special
It makes me feel wonderful

Hugs and kisses to you both
I send you all my love

My Dear Christina

How are you now
What are you up to

I miss you so much
I can't wait to see you again

I keep your picture
In my locket close to my heart

You are so sweet
I hope you always stay that way

Dear Michael

Hello there Michael
I sure miss you a lot

You are so fun to be around
You make me smile and laugh

Your picture is near my heart
And will stay there forever

I think about you a lot
I hope to see you soon

Tammy Jo

Hello Tammy Jo
I'm thinking about you

You are in my thoughts
And in my heart
So are your sweet kids

I'm so glad we met
I feel close to you

We've known each other
For almost 2 years
But it feels longer

You are special to me
I'll never stop being your friend

Susan, My Friend

Susan this is for you
I love you so much

I can't say enough
Good things about you

You are so special to me
I believe in you and your talent

I'm glad you are my friend
And my honorary sister

I will always be here for you
You are always in my heart

If you need me
You know where I am

My Friend Jennifer

Hey there Jennifer
We've been friends for so long
Almost 8 years now

I feel close to you
Even when we are far apart

I tell you everything
We can talk about anything

Serious conversations are good to have
But our fun ones make me laugh

We have changed as people do
But still remain as close as ever
I hope we remain close forever

Baby Sis Amy

My dearest Amy
I think of you as my baby sis
You are my youngest honorary sister

We've grown very close
I keep your picture near my heart

I think about you every day
And every night too

I am here for you
Now and forever

Tell me anything
I'll listen and help if I can
I love you so much

Hege And Mari

Hello both of you
Do you know how much
You mean to me

Hege and Mari
I have grown close to you
I can't believe you live far away

Your pictures are in my photo album
And will stay there always

I'm so happy I met you
Proud to be your honorary sister
I mean that for both of you

I am here for you both
Now and always
I love you so much

Hello Kelly

Kelly you are amazing
You do so much

You say such nice things to me
And make me feel good

Thank you for being there
Thank you for caring

I'm here for you always
Got a problem tell me
Friends listen to each other

You're a wonderful friend
Please never forget me
I love you more than words can say

Yahya

Hi my dear friend Yahya

I want you to know
I'm thinking about you

I have not known you long
But I am so glad to know you

You are so kind
You make me feel so loved
I can't thank you enough

You are very special to me
So very important to me

Thank you for your friendship
I hope we stay friends forever

Too Many To Name

I have too many friends
To name them all

Having so many friends
Is a wonderful feeling

Susan, everything I have said
I honestly and truly mean

Tammy Jo you are very unique
And will always be in my heart

Christina and Michael
Words can't explain
How very much you mean to me

Jennifer, you have been
My friend longer than anyone

Mari, I love you
Thanks for your support

Hege, you mean so much to me
I hope you know this

Kelly you are amazing
I'm so happy to know you

Aimee, so many e-mails
You are a true friend

Tamanna you are dear to me
Yamileth I miss you
Andrea I'm here for you

Like I said
There are too many friends
Too many to name you all

But I love you all so much
You're always in my heart

Uncle Norm

I didn't want to lose a chance
To let you know how I feel
I care about you so much

You are very important to me
I value your advice

I love talking to you
And having you around

You're special to me
I want you to know that

No matter what happens in life
You'll always be in my heart
Because I love you dearly

Chapter Four

Michael Jackson Poems

These are poems I wrote about Michael Jackson!

Don't Judge Michael Jackson!

I hate when people judge Michael
It makes me so mad

Do you know him
Do you know anything about him

About the plastic surgery
Get over it
It's not your business

What he did or didn't do
So what and who cares

Michael is a brilliant entertainer
And Michael helps many people

I'm not telling you what to think
But stop judging Michael
Leave him alone

Your Music

Your music is powerful
It is inspirational

Your music is advice
As well as encouragement

Your music teaches
Things people need to know

Your music gets me through my pain

It does that for many people

Your music is amazing
Because you are amazing

Your music is the best medicine
That I could ever have

What About Michael

What about Michael Jackson
Is it that I love so much

I don't know
Many things

As an entertainer he is the best
But that isn't the biggest reason

Michael is so gorgeous
Yes I really think so

Michael helps so many people
That includes me

Michael is so amazing
He is kind and generous

What can I say
I love Michael Jackson so much
I wish Michael would give me a hug

In This World

In this world
There is one thing
I want more than anything

That wish is not to feel better
Although I want that too
It's miserable to feel bad all the time

My wish isn't for friends
I got some great ones

Do you want to know my wish
It's to meet you in person

Michael I want to meet you
Talk to you
And become true friends

This is my biggest hope
It keeps me going
When nothing else can

I pray for it every night
I honestly do

I love you Michael Jackson
Please come here and hold me

Michael Keeps Me Going

I know the children
Keep you going

Michael you keep me going
When nothing else can

You bring me hope
I believe in you
You are special

My biggest dream is to meet you
And become a real friend
To you and for you

I honestly love you
I always have and always will

I Need You Michael

You have no idea
Got no clue

That I need you Michael
I can't live without you

You give me hope
I believe in you

You are special
You bring joy into my life

Without your influence
I would give up

You keep me going when nothing can
I want to do the same for you

What I Want, Michael

What I want, Michael
Is very simple
I want friendship

No more than I would give to you
And no less than I would give

My friendship is true
It's always unconditional

I'll be there no matter what
You can tell me your troubles
I will listen without judging

We can have fun together too
No need to be serious all the time

Please think about this request
I love you <u>unconditionally</u>
I'd be a good friend

Proud To Love Michael Jackson

I can honestly say
I'm proud to love Michael Jackson

I don't care what anyone thinks
I'm a Michael Jackson fan

Michael has wonderful songs
They're inspirational

But I love him for who he is
Michael is very caring and generous
He has a wonderful heart

Michael is my inspiration
I admire and believe in Michael

Thank You, Michael

There is so much I'd like to thank you for
I don't know where to begin

Thank you for my friends
Around the world
I wouldn't have met them
If I wasn't a fan of yours

I am proud to be a fan
It makes me feel good inside

Thank you for inspiring me
You keep me going through so much
I want to help heal the world

Thank you for making me happy
My biggest dream is to meet you
Oh Michael, I love you so much!

Dearest Michael

What you mean to me
Isn't easy to explain

It is a powerful feeling
Words are not strong enough

I love you so much
You make me very happy

You help me through my pain
And have helped me make friends

You are special to me
I sincerely care about you

I wish you the best
You deserve it

I believe in you
I support and admire you

You are the greatest
As an artist and a person

My biggest dream is to meet you
I pray for this every night

I hope you will like me
And give me a hug

I send to you sincere love
And heartfelt hugs

Thinking Of You Now

I'm thinking of you right now
I think of you a lot Michael

Thinking of you keeps me going
When I am thinking of you
My thoughts are not on painful things

Thinking of you makes me happy
More than you can imagine

I think of you
Wondering what you are doing
And how you are

I hope you are healthy and happy
I hope your kids are too

Maybe someday you'll think of me too
I really hope so

Keep the faith Michael
Never give up!

Hello Michael

How are you Michael
I hope you are well

I hope your kids are well too
I'm sure they are so sweet

I want to get to know you
To know how you think
And what you feel

You are important to me
Honestly you are

I wish you health
And happiness
Now and always

Don't worry about what others think
You are very special

You are kind and caring
You got a kind heart

Please don't change
I love you the way you are

Chapter Five

Dreams and Other Poems

These are poems about
dreams and other stuff!

Dreams

Some people think dreams are bad
Or a waste of time
I'm not one of them

I believe people need dreams
Dreams give you hope

If you believe in a dream
It can keep you going
Dreams can give you strength
And courage

Dreams can give you a reason
To struggle through your pain
Without a dream you may feel lost

I have dreams of my own
I believe in them
They do everything I mentioned

So if you have a dream
Don't give up on it
A dream can come true
But you got to believe
And try

Last Night

Last night I felt you there
I don't know how or why

I didn't see you

Or hear you
I just felt you

I know you weren't there
So I can't explain it

It was so weird
I do not understand it

Fiction And Poetry

I love to write
Especially fiction and poetry

I started writing fiction stories first
I love fiction best
But I love poetry too

Each have something I enjoy
Poetry expresses how I feel
But I love creating characters

Writing is what I love best
And it's what I do best

I have decided
To try to combine the two

That way I can write poems
And still use my characters

Message To You

Why can't I reach you
How do I get through to you

Can't you see I need you
Don't you feel it

All I want is you
You are what I need most

My hopes and dreams are about you
My thoughts are with you
And about you

Do you understand me
Does this make sense to you
I hope it's clear how I feel

My pain is real
But you make me happy

You make me happier
Than anything else can

And happier than anyone can
I wish you could see that

I wish you were here with me
To hug and hold me
Just to love me

I can't say it better than this
I love you and need you
I hope you get my message soon

My Characters

I was thinking
About characters I created
I realized something

Nick has my confusion
Ritchie has my anger

Johnny has my kindness
Shane has my openness

Angela has my kind heart
Adrian knows what is important

Not all my characters are like me
Some do something I wish I could do

Trisha and Ryan are outspoken
They say exactly what they think

Ty has many sides just like me
One side he shows and one doesn't

Ty saves many lives
I wish I could do that

All my characters
Have some of me in them

Some have my ability
And some have my thoughts

I love writing
And I love my characters

All my characters are fictional
And created by me alone
They are in my fictional stories

Chapter Six

Character Poems

These are poems from my
fictional characters
(that I used in my stories)!
Of course they are
written by me. :)

Characters Talk!

Ritchie: Don't judge me
Nick: It hurts so bad

Ritchie: I ain't stupid
Mikey: We see more than you think

Ty: Don't hurt the children
Johnny: Add peace to the world

Ryan: Don't hide how you feel
Trisha: Speak your thoughts

Andy: Look past what you <u>think</u> you see
Angela: It's easy to love and care

Sara: Love is amazing
Kenny: Love can change your life

Katie: Life can be cruel
Shane: But be open and kind

Adrian: Figure out what is important
Jeremy: Protect each other

Bryce: All you have to do is care
Jerry: It's easy to help others

Nick: Kids are hurting
Johnny: Too much pain

Ty: Why do you abuse and hurt
Angela: We can heal each other
Lisha: Keep your mind and heart open

What Ty Wants

I don't want anything
My brother says I do

All I want, is for my brothers
And children all over

I want children to be happy
Never sad or hurt

Children deserve the best
Make sure you give it to them

Cherish children
That's what they need and deserve

Be good to the children
Or you'll have to deal with me

Ty Pretending

I pretend to be one way
And I am that way

It's easier to pretend
It hides the pain

I will show what's in my heart
But only to those I trust

I act cold
And sure I'm distant

I'm protecting my heart
But I'm protecting you as well

Just because I'm hurting
Does not mean I want to hurt you

Ty Is

I am what I am
And I don't care what anyone thinks

I wear all black
And act the way I want

If you don't like me
I don't care

Don't judge me
And don't get in my face

People have the right to be themself
Without being judged

I won't judge you
So don't bother me

Ty's Concerns

What do we care about
In the world today
What do you care about

I know what I care about

The children

Why do we hurt them
They deserve better

Don't hurt and neglect them
Love and cherish the children

Children are important and special
Treat them with love
And protect them with all you have

Children are more valuable than anything
Remember that

Ty

There are 2 sides of me
Only one will I show

The other I hide
Only those who truly know me
Can ever see it

On the outside I'm hard
I'm living with a broken heart

Been hurt too many times
So I hide how I feel

I don't want anyone to know
That I actually do care

These are my 2 sides

But you'll only see 1
Because it's all I will show

Ty's View

My name is Ty
And I have something to say

It's important
So listen up

Why do you wanna
Mess with people who are different

Differences are superficial
Can't you see that

Why do you hurt the children
Don't you know how special they are
Teach them and love them

I hope you listened and learned
Don't mess with me
Because I do mess back

Lisha Knows

I know things most don't
I listen and pay attention

I stay open to the world around me
I notice things most people just see

You can do all this too
It's very easy

Just keep your eyes open
Be open to new and different things

There are many wonderful things
Be open and you'll discover them

If you close your mind and heart
You lose the joy of life

Nick's Wish

I wish for many things
Everyone has wishes

I want to be taken seriously
And treated fairly

I want to be happy
I want to be loved

I want to help people
And to make a difference

I want to be a regular kid
But I want to be more than a kid

I wish people would stop judging me
It hurts to be judged

Nick's Goal

Some people don't take kids seriously
My goal is to change that

So what if I'm a kid
I still want to be taken seriously

I have thoughts and opinions
Dreams and goals

I want to show people
Kids are important too

I have things I want to do
And things to accomplish

Everyone is important
So please don't underestimate kids

Nick's Thoughts

People say I'm a cute little boy
But I'm not a little boy

I know I'm 10 years old
But I'm more than that

I'm a person too
With hopes and fears

I feel things as strong as you do
Don't underestimate me
Just because I'm young

I got things I wanna do
I'd like to help people

I've been told to follow my dreams
And that's what I'm gonna do
You should too

Nick Talks

My big brother taught me everything
He taught me what's important

I know what's important
And I know what I want

Love is a gift
It's a special gift

Everyone needs it
And everyone deserves it

Don't spend time hating
Use that time to love

Why cause pain
When you could help to heal

Johnny's Plan

I have a plan
Of things I wanna do

I want to help people

Teach them to be more loving

I believe every person is special
All people are important

I've been told I have a good heart
And I'm very proud of that

I think most people are loving
But some are afraid to show it

It really is easy to love and care
So please try it, okay

Johnny Wants

I know what I want
Do you know what you want

I want to help people
I wanna make people happy

I enjoy loving people
Loving is important

Every person is special
Unique too

All people are important
Everyone deserves love

I don't know you
But I love you anyway

Johnny's Voice

I don't understand
Why people judge and hate

It's true I'm just 8
But isn't it important to love

Doesn't it make you feel good
When you help someone

I'm very loving
And that feels good

It's easy to love people
And it makes you feel good
Way down deep in your heart

Ryan says

I may be young
But I know what's important

Love is the most important thing
Remember that

Love freely
And unconditionally

Have an open mind
And a giving heart

I don't hide how I feel

I speak my mind
I know what's important to me
Do you know what's important to you

Ryan's Attitude

I'm not a serious person
But I can be serious

I prefer to enjoy things
I live carefree

I'm serious when I need to be
But when I don't I'm not

I'm not afraid to say what I feel
I say what I think

I wanna be a kid
Because by age I am a kid

I live my life with love and fun
You should do the same

Shane Believes

What do I believe in
I believe in a lot of things

I believe in my brothers
Younger and older

I believe in children

All children
I believe in dreams
They truly are important

I believe in my heart
Everyone should follow their heart

Do you have something you believe in
I really hope you do

Shane Thinking

People say I'm just a kid
I say 14 is not just a kid

Sure I got the heart of a kid
But I believe I always will

I may be seen as a kid
But I'm very mature
Too mature I've been told

I'm easy going
And easy to get along with

I don't judge
I just love
Ain't that how I should be

Trisha Cares

I care about many things

Everyone should
I care about everyone I love
Loved ones are important

I care about the children
Of the world

All children are important
You need to know that

Let's care about the important things
Not unimportant things

Don't waste time on hate
Use your heart to love

Trisha's Love

I know what I think and how I feel
And I know who I love

I love my family
And my boyfriend and his family

Love is awesome
And it's powerful

Love is special
And wonderful

Do you have someone you love
Cherish them with all your heart

I let my heart guide me

I always have and always will

Ritchie's Pain

Why don't you take the time
To understand

You don't know me
Well enough to judge me

Did I hurt you
No, so why do you hurt me

I may be different than you
That doesn't make me bad

There are more important things
Than judging me or anyone else

Why can't you understand
Just leave me alone

Ritchie Talking

Sure I'm angry
So what

I think you'd be angry too
If you were misjudged
And treated bad

I am the way I am
That don't give you the right to judge

So what if you don't understand
I don't understand you either
Don't judge me
Just let me be me
And I'll let you be you

Mikey Needs

Everyone needs something
Isn't it true

I need things too
I'm no different that you
Well at least not much

What I need most
Is love and to be cared about

Everyone needs to be loved
Love is more important than anything

I have love and give love
I hope you do too

Mikey Speaks

I may be a kid at 11 years old
But I know what I want

I know what I think
And how I feel

I got opinions too

Doesn't everyone

What's important about differences
We are all unique

Everyone is special
We all have different views

So please try to love
Be open and don't judge

Angela's Advice

I'm going to give you advice
This advice comes from my heart

It's important to be open
And equally important to love

Love is powerful
It can heal the pain inside

Listen to your heart
Follow your heart

You can achieve anything you want
Everyone can

You have to make it happen
Don't just wait go for it

Angela's Heart

What you really need
In this world is love
Love is all that's important
Love others freely

You need to follow your heart
Let your feelings show

Let your heart inspire you
And let it guide you

It never hurts to care
Always Love from your heart
And with all your heart

Jeremy's Turn

I'm very loving
And I am protective

Maybe I'm overprotective
It's because I care so much

You can never care too much
That's my belief

Love and understanding
That's what everyone needs

Cherish the people you love
They are important
Always remember that

Bryce's Feelings

It's a hard world
That doesn't mean you got to be hard

It's important to care
And to show you care

Loving is easy
And love is beautiful

Be sincere
Never just pretend

Be open and kind
And honestly care

Hating helps no one
Loving helps everyone

Adrian Saying

What do I want
You wanna know

I'm a 19 year old guy
And I want to live my life
I want to be myself
Without being judged

I wish for love
I want to be happy

Everyone has the right

To live their own life

You don't need to understand
Just let it be

Andy Sees

You act like you don't care
But I see through that

I can read people
I've been doing it for years
Since I was a kid

I know you're hurting
Don't pretend you're not
You can not fool me

There is so much pain
Everyone feels some

But don't freeze your heart
It is important to care

Sara Speaks Up

I'm a 12 year old girl
Yeah sure that's young
But it doesn't mean
I don't feel things

I know my heart
I know who I love

And who I admire

I do not know
What I want to be

But I'll figure it out
Then I will achieve it

Katie's Poem

I know I'm 15
And that seems young

But I have experienced a lot
I've seen a lot of things
More than some people twice my age

I know what's important in life
And know first hand about the pain

Life is full of surprises
Anything can happen

Take my advice
Experience the good
And get through the bad

Kenny's Opinion

I know I am a kid
People say 12 is a kid

But I'm so much more
Please don't limit what I can do

I have a heart and a mind
Just the same as everyone

I know what I think
I know how I feel

I have my own dreams
I will accomplish many things
Throughout my life

Chapter Seven

About The Author

About me!!

About The Author

This is Selena Millman. I was born on June 22, 1973 in Cleveland Ohio. I started writing in 1983.

I like to describe my beginning of writing as I had a strong idea that I couldn't get rid of so I started writing. With practice I figured out what I was doing and what I wanted to do. I started writing stories, then poems, lyrics, essays, and then short stories.

I write whatever inspires me. I'd love to create movies and a play. I put my thoughts and emotions into my writing. I can't write it if I don't feel it!

Well I hope you enjoy reading this. And maybe it touched you just a little. I hope you think about what I said. Remember anything is possible. Just believe and don't give up!

Love and Peace,

Selena Millman

Places you can help and get help:
http://www.geocities.com/Paris/Rue/6184/Help2.html

My characters:
http://www.geocities.com/Paris/Rue/6184/characters.html

Dedication

I dedicate this to all my friends that I love and hold dear. Jennifer, Susan, Mari, Hege, Tammy Jo, Amy, Luciana, Andrea, Aimee, Yamileth, Tamanna, Kelly, Sandra, Sara, Michelle, and Reva you are my honorary sisters! Thank you for being my friends. You're in my heart. I love you 24/7!!

Christina and Michael I want you to know I enjoy being your honorary auntie and I will always love you. You are very special to me!

Monica, Hanna, Yahya, Jason, Alejandra, Jodie, Kelli, Maria, Jackie, Leslie Ann, Jamie, Indra, Kim, Donna and Sharde you mean a lot to me as well.

To all of my friends, your friendship means so much to me. You all believe in me when I might not. You give me my strength! I value your friendship! You mean more to me than my words can express. I will always be here for all of you!

Uncle Norm, thank you for all of your advice, support, and encouragement. I truly appreciate it!

I also dedicate this to everyone I love and everyone who loves me. You know who you are. You are the special ones in my life. Love is the most important thing in life.

Note to Michael Jackson:

Michael, I want you to know all this is true. Everything I say is how I honestly feel.

I don't say it if I don't mean it. What's the point of that? The way I say I feel is the way I honestly feel!!

I have been a fan since 1983. Nothing and no one will change my love for you. As an artist no one will ever be better than you. You're the best.

Keep the faith Michael! I don't think you are strange. I think you are a genius. You have a kind heart. Don't lose that and please don't change!

I hope all your dreams come true. You deserve it. Take good care of yourself and your kids!

Maybe someday my dream will come true and we can meet face to face. Forgive me if I'm shy when that happens.

I love you so very much! You have been the biggest influence on me. I've dreamt of meeting you for years now. I honestly am here for you.

Love and Peace to You Always!

With Love,
Selena Millman
from the USA
December 3, 1999